Speaking better English

Lernwortschatz für die
mündliche Kommunikation

Dr. Rolf Giese
Eckhard Schroeder
Christoph Wurm

Ernst Klett Sprachen
Stuttgart

1. Auflage   1   14 13 12 11 10 | 2026 25 24 23 22

Autoren: Dr. Rolf Giese, Eckhard Schroeder, Christoph Wurm
Konzeption: Christoph Wurm

Sprecher/innen: Debby Böhm, Beth Jarvis-Silliman, Edith Michaelsen, Paul Newcomb, Astrid Proctor, Sebastian Schmitt
Tonaufnahmen: andreas nesic, custom music, Stuttgart

Redaktion: Debby Böhm
Layoutkonzeption: Ulrike Wollenberg
Gestaltung und Satz: Satzkasten, Stuttgart
Umschlaggestaltung und Mediengestaltung: Sandra Vrabec
Druck und Bindung: Salzland Druck, Staßfurt

Printed in Germany
ISBN 978-3-12-519571-4

Lernen mit *Speaking better English*

Wer?

Als Ergänzung zum beliebten Lernwortschatz *Writing better English* rückt *Speaking better English* den mündlichen Sprachgebrauch in den Mittelpunkt. Das Buch wendet sich an alle Benutzer der englischen Sprache – Lernende wie Lehrende.

Es umfasst alltägliche Gesprächssituationen im privaten Bereich, die geschäftliche Kommunikation in unmittelbaren Begegnungen oder am Telefon, professionell vorbereitete Präsentationen, die Leitung von Diskussionsrunden oder auch die gezielte Vorbereitung auf Bewerbungsgespräche und mündliche Prüfungen in Schule und Hochschule.

Speaking better English ist daher eine praktische und benutzerfreundliche Hilfe für
- das allgemeine Auffrischen und Vertiefen des gesprochenen Englisch
- den konkreten Gebrauch im englischsprachigen Ausland
- den Umgang mit englischsprachigen Gästen im deutschen Sprachraum
- den zielgerichteten Gebrauch im internationalen Geschäftsbereich
- die Anwendung im schulischen Unterricht bereits ab der Sekundarstufe I
- die ausführliche Vorbereitung auf mündliche Prüfungen für Schüler und Studierende
- Sprachkurse in der Erwachsenenbildung

Was?

Speaking better English enthält – nach zentralen Kompetenzen geordnet – die wichtigsten ca. 1500 Vokabeln, Ausdrücke und Wendungen, die zur aktiven Gestaltung verschiedener mündlicher Kommunikationssituationen benötigt werden. Die Gliederung orientiert sich an gängigen Gesprächskonstellationen und erleichtert zielgerichtetes Lernen in übersichtlichen, in sich geschlossenen Einheiten.

In der modernen Fremdsprachendidaktik ist die mündliche Kommunikation von elementarer Bedeutung. Klassenarbeiten und Klausuren werden verstärkt durch mündliche Prüfungen ersetzt. Speziell der Vorbereitung und Durchführung von *Oral Exams* ist daher ein ausführliches Kapitel gewidmet. Es basiert auf den aktuellen Lehrplänen der ausgehenden Sekundarstufe I und orientiert sich an den neuen kompetenzorientierten Vorgaben für das Zentralabitur. Einen genaueren Einblick in die konkrete Durchführung von mündlichen Prüfungen geben modellhafte Beispiele.

Wie?

Speaking better English eignet sich sowohl für den Einsatz im Unterricht als auch zum gezielten Selbststudium. Ferner ist das Buch ein nützlicher Begleiter auf Reisen ins englischsprachige Ausland sowie eine praktische Hilfe bei verschiedenen internationalen Begegnungen.

Das Lernen und Anwenden des Sprachmaterials erfolgt in einfachen und klaren Schritten. Jede Seite ist zweigeteilt: In der linken, breiteren Spalte werden die Vokabeln und Redewendungen im Satzzusammenhang präsentiert, der englische Lernwortschatz ist dabei fett gedruckt. Rechts befinden sich die deutschen Übersetzungen. Die konkrete Einbettung in Satzstrukturen dient dazu, Fehler bei der Anwendung von Begriffen und Wendungen zu vermeiden.

Zur genaueren Erläuterung sowohl grammatischer Eigenarten als auch Besonderheiten bei der Intonation dienen die *Info-Boxes*. Für das gezielte Üben der korrekten Aussprache bietet *Speaking better English* spezielles Audiomaterial, welches von *native speakers* präsentiert wird. Um die Audiodateien und deren Transkripte abzurufen, scannen Sie einfach den QR-Code der jeweiligen Seite und hören Sie sich die Beispieldialoge an oder laden Sie sie herunter. Alternativ können Sie den Code, den Sie unter dem QR-Code sehen, auf www.klett-sprachen.de in das Suchfeld eingeben. Sie werden dann auf die *Speaking better English – audio online'* Seite geleitet. Dort können Sie sich die Dateien anhören oder herunterladen. Die beiden Register (Englisch und Deutsch) am Ende des Buches ermöglichen das rasche Auffinden von Vokabeln und Redewendungen.

Um Doppelungen bei der Übersetzung von *you* zu vermeiden, wird in der Regel die 2. Person Singular *Du* verwendet. Bei eher förmlichen Ausdrücken und Wendungen erfolgt die deutsche Übersetzung mit *Sie*.

Contents

Abkürzungen

AE – American English   etw. – etwas
BE – British English   jmd. – jemandem
coll – colloquial
fml – formal
inf – informal
sb – somebody
sth – something

Hi, I'm Eleanor. Nice to meet you.

Hi. I'm Peter. You look very familiar. Have we met before?

I don't think so. But now that you mention it….

Did you go to last year's conference in Bristol?

Yes, I did. Oh, now I remember! You were at the bookstand, weren't you?

Yes, I was. Well, it's nice to meet you again.

And you. Sorry about not recognizing you earlier.

…

1.1 Meeting people / Introducing yourself – Leute treffen / Sich vorstellen

> Both in Britain and in the US, most people do not shake hands every time they meet, but only when they meet for the first time. The expression *from the moment we shook hands* means *from the moment we met for the first time*.

Good morning,	Mr Bertram.	Guten Morgen
Good afternoon,	madam.	Guten Tag
Good evening,	sir.	Guten Abend
How do you do, *(fml)*		Guten Tag

Hello,		
Hi,	Jane.	Hallo.
Hey, *(inf)*		
Hiya, *(inf)*		

Excuse me,	are you Mrs Carpenter?	
Sorry,	you are Mr Field, aren't you?	Entschuldigung, …
Pardon my asking *(fml),*	you must be the new caretaker.	Verzeihung
Hello,		

			(sich / jemanden vorstellen)
May I			Darf ich
Let me		myself.	Lassen Sie mich
	introduce	my colleague, Stephanie.	vorstellen
I just want to		a friend of mine.	Ich möchte gerade / nur
Please, allow me to *(fml)*			Bitte erlauben Sie, dass
I would like to *(fml)*			Ich würde gern

I'm		
My name is	Patrick.	Ich heiße
This is		Das ist

I'm from		Ich bin aus
I come from		Ich komme aus
I was born in	Chicago.	Ich wurde geboren in
I grew up in		Ich bin aufgewachsen in
My family is from		Meine Familie kommt aus

	twenty-two years old.		
	a student at Columbia University.		Ich bin …
I'm	**doing my A-levels** at Paisley Grammar School.		mache gerade mein Abitur
	here on	**a business trip.**	Geschäftsreise
		holiday. *(BE)*	Urlaub
		vacation. *(AE)*	

How	are you? are things? 're you doing? *(inf)* 's it going? *(inf)*	Wie geht es dir?

(Are) you (Is) everything	all right? *(inf)* ok? *(inf)*	(Ist) alles in Ordnung?

It's	a pleasure very nice great		freut mich schön großartig
Pleased I'm delighted		**to meet** you.	kennenlernen erfreut sein

There is sb I'd like you	to meet. to get to know a little more.	kennenlernen etwas besser kennenlernen

I	think assume don't think	we've met before. we've **actually** met.	glaube vermute wirklich

Have we Have you two	met before?	Haben wir uns Sind Sie (beide) sich

It's been	a long time quite a while two years ages	since we last met.	eine längere Zeit ziemlich lange zwei Jahre außerordentlich lange

What are	you	up to? planning now? doing around here?	vorhaben, beabsichtigen
	your	plans?	

What have you **been up to**?	gemacht, angestellt

Please note the following points about greetings in English: Conversation starters such as *Hello! How are you?* are rather common at informal as well as formal meetings. Generally, *How are you?* is not meant as a question enquiring about a person's health. Long answers or explanations are not expected in English. A standard answer is *Fine, thanks,* which is frequently followed by *And how are you?* or *What about you?*

1.2 Being polite – Höflich sein

Using *please* and *thank you* is essential when you want to be polite. In a conversation it may be considered rude if you leave out the word *please*.
Grammatically speaking, *please* can be used in different parts of the sentence, either at the beginning, before the verb, or at the end. Make sure you stress the word *please* if you want to give more emphasis to your request.

> *Please* can you explain this again?
> Can you *please* explain this again?
> Can you explain this again, *please*?

Remember that the word *please* at the beginning of a sentence is frequently used as an order and not as a polite request.

Excuse me, **Sorry,**	can I help you?	Entschuldigung

Can I			können
May I	book		dürfen
Is it ok with you if I		a table for lunch on Sunday?	angenehm sein
Would it be all right if I booked			Wäre es in Ordnung, wenn ich …

Wouldn't you like to			
Would you like to			
Why don't you	join	us for dinner tonight?	Würdest du gern
Why not *(inf)*			
How about joining			

Is it	**convenient if I** *(fml)* **possible to**	take a look at the apartment now, please?	möglich sein, können
Can I			
May I			können, dürfen

I	**wondered** **was wondering**	if you were free this evening.	sich fragen, überlegen

I would	**very much like** **love**	you to watch the show with us.	sich wünschen

I	would	**appreciate it very much** *(fml)* **be very glad**	if you could come to the party on Saturday.	sich sehr freuen
It would be great				es wäre großartig

(sich erkundigen)

What are you doing		on Wednesday afternoon? at the weekend?	Was machst du
Are you	**busy**		Bist du beschäftigt
	free	tomorrow?	frei
	available		verfügbar

Do you want		to meet		Möchtest du gerne
Would you like			the artist after the show?	Würdest du gerne
Do you	**fancy** *(inf)*			
	feel like	meeting		Ist dir danach
Are you up to *(inf)*				

(jemanden um einen Gefallen bitten)

Can I ask you to		Kann ich dich
Could you (possibly)		Könntest du vielleicht
I was wondering if you could		Ich habe mich gefragt, ob
	do me a **favour**? / .	Gefallen

(freundlich anbieten)

Why don't I	**give you**	my cell phone number.	Warum gebe ich dir nicht
Let me		my e-mail address.	Lass mich dir … geben

(vorschlagen)

Let's			Lasst uns
I think we should			Ich finde wir sollten
Why don't we	have	a drink first. / ?	Warum (gehen) wir nicht
We could always			Wir könnten
How about having			Wie wär's mit

(sich mit dem Partner freuen)

	happy		sich freuen
I'm (very / really)	**pleased**	to hear that.	
	glad		glücklich sein
	delighted		erfreut, entzückt sein

(Mitgefühl ausdrücken)

I'm	**really**	**sorry**	about what happened to your dog.
	so		for your loss.

Es tut mir sehr / so leid.

		feel	**bad.**	schlecht
I don't want you	**to**		**distressed.**	bekümmert
		be	**unhappy.**	unglücklich
			upset.	bestürzt

(beruhigen, beschwichtigen)

Don't	**worry**, Mrs. Cahill!
	let it worry you!
Not to	**worry**, Sam!
Please	**calm down**, sir!

Machen Sie sich keine Sorgen
Lassen Sie sich nicht beunruhigen
Keine Sorge
(sich) beruhigen

(sich entschuldigen)

I	**'d like to**	**apologize for**	
	want to		my long absence.
Let me			
Please **forgive** me for			

Ich möchte mich gern
  entschuldigen für
Erlauben Sie mir
verzeihen

(sich mit Bedauern entschuldigen)

I	deeply sincerely *(fml)*	regret	that I won't be able to accompany you on the trip to Dublin.
Let me express my regret *(fml)*			for not responding to your message.

Ich bedaure sehr

Ich bedaure ausdrücklich

(sich bedanken)
Herzlichen Dank

Thank you	very much (indeed)!
	ever so much for your **hospitality**!
	in advance!

Thanks a million. *(inf)*

Thanks	**again.**
	all the same.
	anyway.

Thanks, I **appreciate** it.

Gastfreundschaft
im Voraus
tausend Dank
noch einmal
trotzdem
trotzdem
etw. zu schätzen wissen

I'll	**return the favour** sometime.
	do the same for you one day.
I	(really) **owe** you
	one.
	a favour.

sich revanchieren,
einen Gefallen tun

jemandem etwas schuldig sein

When responding to someone who says *Thank you!*, German learners of English tend to make mistakes. *Bitte sehr* cannot be translated with *please*! The most common responses to *Thank You!* are *You're welcome, Don't mention it , Not at all,* or *No problem*. A more informal expression is, for example, *Not to worry. No worries* or *No sweat!* are even more informal.

1.3 Keeping the conversation going – Das Gespräch am Laufen halten

One of the most essential grammatical devices to keep a conversation going in English is the use of **question tags**. They are used very frequently in spoken English but never in (written) formal English. Question tags are short additions to sentences asking for a direct comment from your conversation partner. They are always used in the **contracted form**. The subject of the question tag is always a pronoun, never a noun. The German translation can be *nicht wahr?* or *oder?*

When the sentence is affirmative, the question tag is in the negative interrogative form:

Sandra went to Madrid, did**n't** she? – Yes, she did.
The Thompsons are Welsh, are**n't** they? – Yes, they are.
I can borrow your car, ca**n't** I? – Yes, you can.

When the sentence is negative, the question tag is in the familiar interrogative form:

Pythons do**n't** make good pets, do they? – No, they don't.
Young people should**n't** drive so fast, should they? – No, they shouldn't.
You have**n't** been in town for a while, have you? – No, I haven't.

Please note that the **intonation** you use with a question tag indicates the level of certainty in your statement.

Be careful when using **question tags** with **modal verbs**. If there is a modal verb in the main part of the sentence, the modal verb has to be used in the question tag.

> She **must** be eighteen now, **mustn't** she?
> He **will** take the new job in Washington, **won't** he?

Another common way of keeping a conversation going by expressing your particular interest in what your partner is saying is the use of **short question forms**, which repeat what has been said by a person. This encourages a further exchange.

I'm going to take part in a global conference on sustainability.	**Are you?**
We managed to get two tickets for the FA Cup Final.	**Did you?**
I try to keep fit by going to the gym four times a week.	**Do you?**

In these cases be careful with the intonation. Make sure that you stress the verb form in a way that expresses your surprise and real interest in your partner's statement. Otherwise, your question could be understood as an ironic remark.

Did you know that Susan and Phil are getting married in June?	**Really?**		Tatsächlich?
	That's	**interesting!**	interessant
		amazing!	erstaunlich
	How	**exciting!**	Wie aufregend!
		wonderful!	Wunderbar!
	Wow! (inf)		
My sister Liz has finally finished her A-levels.	That's **brilliant news!**		großartige Neuigkeiten
	Congratulations!		Glückwunsch!
	Fantastic!		fantastisch
	That's	**marvellous!**	herrlich
		splendid!	großartig
Dr Steptoe is a brilliant surgeon.	**That's true.**		
	Absolutely!		auf jeden Fall
	Definitely!		
Families should spend more time together.	That's	**very true!**	*(zustimmen)* stimmt genau
		exactly what I think!	genau was ich denke
	I	absolutely fully **agree.**	zustimmen
		couldn't **agree** more.	
		know what you mean.	ich verstehe, was du meinst

(Meinung erfragen)

What	should be done	about	legalizing certain drugs in California?	Was soll man tun
	do you think			Wie denkst du über
	view do you take on			Was ist deine Sicht zu

Where do you **draw the line?** — die Grenze ziehen

(nach Einschätzungen fragen)

How do you feel		about		your new job in Dubai?	Wie geht's dir mit
Are you	excited				aufgeregt
	looking forward	to starting			sich auf etw freuen
How committed are you		to			Wie überzeugt bist du von

(um Erläuterungen bitten)

So when did you	decide to look for a new job?	Wann hast du beschlossen
Are you going to	move to Leeds?	Wirst du
What are your	motives	for	leaving the company?	Beweggrund, Motiv
	plans		the next few months?	Plan, Absicht

(auffordern, anregen)

Why	don't you			Warum schreibst du nicht
	doesn't he	write	a letter to the editor?	
Shall we				Sollen wir
Let's				Lass uns
How about writing				Wie wär's wenn

(darum bitten, Konsequenzen bedenken)

Just	think of	the consequences.	bedenken
	consider		berücksichtigen
	imagine		sich vorstellen

What will happen if we don't try to save the environment? — Was wird passieren

(Vorschlag machen)

Wouldn't it	be	good to	get a new smartphone? / .	Wäre es nicht gut / besser
		better to		Wäre es nicht sinnvoller
	make more sense to			Du solltest besser
You'd	better			Du solltest lieber
	rather			

(empfehlen, vorschlagen)

You	need to	change		Du musst
	might want to			Du solltest vielleicht
I would recommend				Ich würde empfehlen
We should think about	changing	the layout. / ?		Wir sollten darüber nachdenken
How about				Wie wäre es, wenn

(Unverständnis ausdrücken)

I don't quite	see	what you're	referring to.
	get		driving at.
		your point.	
	understand	you completely.	

sehen

verstehen

What exactly are you trying to say?

Was genau

Maybe
Perhaps
Possibly

vielleicht,
möglicherweise

I	'm **not sure if**	you should ask for a pay rise.
	doubt if	
	wonder if	

sich nicht sicher sein
bezweifeln
sich fragen

If you ask me,
Personally speaking,
Frankly,

I think you should consider the offer very carefully.

Wenn du mich fragst, …
Ganz persönlich gefragt, …
Offen gesagt, …

| **To be** | **frank,** |
| | **quite honest,** |

Um direkt zu sein
Um ganz ehrlich zu sein

Let's look at this	**from a different**	**angle.**
		point of view.
	in several stages.	

unter einem anderen Blick-
winkel betrachten
in mehreren Schritten

Just a	**minute,**
	second,
One moment,	
Hold on, please,	
Hang on *(inf)*,	

there is a final aspect that is of special interest.
I'll check it for you.

einen Augenblick bitte

(positive Aspekte herausstellen)

| **On the** | **other hand,** |
| | **positive side,** |

Andererseits

Then again,
What I like about this,
On second thoughts,

the project in India is doing very well.

Dann wiederum
Was mir daran gefällt
Nach reiflicher Überlegung

(Füllwörter)

So,
Well,
Ok,
Oh yes,
Right,
Anyway,
Anyhow,
And then,
Where was I,
Getting back to my example,

these figures prove a steady rise
in car sales.

also
nun
OK
Oh ja
Richtig

auf jeden Fall

Und dann
Wo war ich
Um auf mein Beispiel
zurückkommen

As I was saying
What I was saying was

Wie schon gesagt

1.4 Being more idiomatic by using phrasal verbs – Flüssiger sprechen durch den Gebrauch von *phrasal verbs*

> **Phrasal verbs** are verbs which are followed by prepositions or adverbs. Native speakers make use of **phrasal verbs** extensively in everyday conversations. Although they are also used in written English, they are mostly avoided in academic writing.
> Generally speaking, using **phrasal verbs** helps to make your spoken English more fluent and idiomatic. **Phrasal verbs** can have very specific meanings, which often differ greatly from the original use of the verb.

The meeting tomorrow has to be **called off.**	absagen
I'll **call you up** as soon as I'm back from Rome.	anrufen
Can I **call you back** in a minute?	zurückrufen
Right after I had **checked into** the hotel, I got a call from my boss.	in ein Hotel einchecken
Let's **check our luggage in** and go to the boarding area.	Gepäck einchecken
Tonight we'll **check out** the new oyster bar in Dean Street.	ausprobieren, prüfen
Where do you **come from**?	herkommen
The whole truth will **come out** at the trial.	herauskommen
You won't believe what I **came across** when I tidied up the attic!	zufällig finden
Please, **drop by** on your way back from work!	vorbeikommen, besuchen
Shall I **drop you off** at the cinema?	aussteigen lassen, absetzen
Did you hear that Sam **has dropped out** of school?	verlassen
Be careful, don't **fall down** the stairs!	herunterfallen
The chocolate cake **fell apart** when it was taken out of the oven.	auseinanderfallen, zerbrechen
The couple **fell out with** each other just before the wedding.	sich streiten
How are you **getting on** at your new school, Kevin?	vorankommen, zurechtkommen
I'm still wondering how the bank robbers **got away**.	entkommen
Do you think Jenny will **get back** to Nottingham?	zurückkommen
It's a shame that Juliet had to **give up** her job at the Foreign Office.	aufgeben
John **gave the money back** to the woman who had lost it.	zurückgeben
At first Mr Webster was reluctant, but then he **gave in**.	nachgeben
Let's **go over** the details of our plan again.	noch einmal anschauen
Hector **went on** working as if nothing had happened.	fortfahren mit
The index of industrial production has **gone up** by 9 per cent since last year.	ansteigen

Please **hang on**, I'll be with you in a second!	warten, am Telefon bleiben
After she had **hung up**, she felt sorry about what she had said.	auflegen, Gespräch beenden
I don't want Dennis to **hang out** with those guys!	Zeit verbringen mit
Keep on trying! Please don't give up!	weitermachen
I'm not sure if I can **keep this from** my parents any longer.	verbergen, zurückhalten
Let's hope the sunny weather **keeps up** for a while.	unverändert bleiben
Hey, **look at** that beautiful red dress over there!	anschauen
I've been **looking for** my wedding ring all day. I can't find it.	suchen
Everyone is really **looking forward to** the Christmas break.	sich freuen auf
Peter keeps **putting off** his appointment.	aufschieben
Don't you think she's **put on** too much make-up?	auftragen
Don't worry, we can easily **put you up** for the night.	unterbringen
Yesterday I **ran into** my old English teacher at the cinema.	zufällig treffen
Mrs Robson's dog was **run over** by a car this morning.	überfahren
We've **run out** of milk. Sally, would you go to the supermaket, please?	nicht mehr haben
He **took** the laptop **apart** and quickly solved the problem.	auseinanderbauen
Hurry up, the plane **takes off** in 20 minutes!	starten
Everybody says that James **takes after** his father.	ähneln
The manager **turned down** his request for a day off.	ablehnen
She waited for half an hour, but he didn't **turn up**.	kommen
Turn off the TV please! Dinner's ready!	ausschalten
He **works out** three times a week in the gym.	trainieren
Before we go on holiday, let's **work out** the total cost!	zusammenstellen, durchrechnen
Sometimes there are days when everything **works out** fine!	gelingen

Three classic pronunciation mistakes made by German speakers
1. The last sound in *of* is not [f] but [v].
2. In most cases, the **s** in the plural or the third person singular is not [s] but [z]: *boy**s** and girl**s**, father**s** and son**s**, she listen**s***; [s] is only used after a voiceless consonant: *he si**t**s, she sto**p**s, than**k**s.*
3. The **a** in words such as *m**a**n, c**a**t, th**a**t, r**a**n, f**a**mily, b**a**d*, is not pronounced [e] but [æ].

1.5 Expressing dislike and annoyance – Missfallen und Verärgerung ausdrücken

I don't	like enjoy care for get much out of	classical music	mögen Freude haben sich nichts daraus machen nicht viel sagen

I'm **not**	very terribly particularly		nicht besonders
		fond of keen on	fast food.	mögen schätzen

I'm	fed up with tired sick (inf) sick and tired (inf)	of working every weekend.	leid sein, satt haben
I don't **appreciate** I can't **accept** I'm not **buying** (inf)	that.		gar nicht gut finden nicht akzeptieren können nicht glauben, nicht abkaufen

You're	missing the point, not getting this (inf),		nicht ganz verstehen
Look,		everyone says it's a bad idea.	Schau
I don't think you	realise that understand that		Du verstehst wohl nicht,

			(höfliche, aber bestimmte Aufforderung)
It would be good **I wonder**	if you could tidy	up your room now. / ?	Es wäre gut, wenn Ich frage mich, ob
Would	you mind	tidying not interrupting me?	Würde es dir etwas ausmachen
Would it be possible for you to stop smoking?			Wäre es möglich / Könntest du bitte

Do you really think you **Are you sure** you	should ought to		Solltest du wirklich Bist du sicher
Isn't it	a **silly** idea to **rather stupid** to **unreasonable** to	make a complaint?	dumm, albern ziemlich unklug unvernünftig

That may be true sometimes,	**but** (even) **though**		aber obwohl
That's true.	**However,** **Even so,**	this is different.	Trotzdem, jedoch Auch wenn, selbst wenn es so ist

			(ironischer Ausdruck von Verärgerung)
Oh	**terrific,** **great,** **brilliant,**	that's just what I need!	toll großartig hervorragend
Of course, you're the expert.			natürlich, selbstverständlich

		(Verärgerung mit Understatement)
That	isn't very **helpful!**	hilfreich
	's **hardly polite!**	kaum höflich
	's **rather nasty!**	ziemlich gemein

Don't		make a fool of yourself!	Mach dich nicht lächerlich!
	be	such a fool! ridiculous! stupid! silly!	Sei nicht { so ein Dummkopf! lächerlich dumm albern

You	**always** leave a mess in the kitchen!		immer, ständig
	never help me with anything!		niemals
I	**hate** **can't stand**	the way you always boss me around!	hassen nicht ertragen können

I think you should	**take that back!** **take back what you've just said!**		etwas zurücknehmen (was gerade gesagt wurde)
I'm not going to let you	**talk to me** like **get away with**	that!	mit sich reden lassen etwas durchgehen lassen

You	're not being **honest!**		ehrlich
	can be	very annoying!	ärgerlich, lästig
		really mean!	böse, gemein

Oh	no, dear,		Oh nein!
Damn *(coll)*,			Verdammt!
For	goodness God's heaven's *(inf)* Pete's *(inf)*	sake,	why does this always happen to me?	Um Himmels willen!

That's	**complete**	nonsense! rubbish! *(inf)*	völliger Unsinn
	absurd!		absurd, aberwitzig
	totally unfair		völlig ungerecht
It's	just simply	**not fair**	to charge us another 500 dollars!	einfach nicht richtig
	preposterous *(fml.)*		absurd
	absolutely ridiculous		völlig lächerlich

1.6 Finishing a conversation – Ein Gespräch beenden

Goodbye,	Mrs Fisher!		Auf Wiedersehen!
Bye-bye, *(inf)*	everybody!		
So long, *(AE, inf)*	Henry!		Tschüss!

Cheerio! *(BE, inf)*

See you	**tomorrow,**	children!	Bis morgen.
	tonight,	Simon!	Bis heute Abend!
	later!		Bis später!
	soon!		Bis bald!
	at eight!		
	at work!		Wir sehen uns um … / bei …
	at the party!		

(plötzlichen Aufbruch ankündigen)

Oh, it's time to go.			Oh, es ist Zeit zu gehen.
Let's make a move *(inf)***!**			Lass uns aufbrechen.
Well then,	**we should be leaving now**.		wir sollten jetzt gehen
Right,	**we are going to leave**.		wir gehen jetzt
Anyway,	**I'm off now!**		Ich bin jetzt weg.
I'm	afraid,	I've got to	**head off** *(inf)***!**	sich auf den Weg machen
	sorry,		**dash off** *(inf)***!**	losflitzen
			rush off *(inf)***!**	eilen

(sich freundlich, höflich verabschieden)

	lovely	to see you!	schön
	good		gut
It's been	wonderful	**to catch up** on old times.	an etwas anknüpfen
	so nice	to meet you.	so schön
	a pleasure		ein Vergnügen

(sich mit guten Wünschen verabschieden)

	good	**day!**	schönen Tag
		time!	Zeit
		one *(AE, inf)***!**	schönen Tag
Have a	**nice afternoon!**		schönen Nachmittag
	great weekend!		tolles Wochenende
	wonderful evening!		wundervollen Abend

Enjoy	your	trip to Paris!	Genieß
		holidays!	

9z58sx

Good morning, everybody.

Good morning, Mr Black.

Christine, could you please close the window and turn on the light?

Yes, of course.

And then I'd like you all to get out your books and turn to page 75. We're going to read chapter 6 together today.

Excuse me, could you repeat that please?

Page 75. OK. I'd like you to get together in groups of four. Take turns and read the chapter out loud to each other. One of you should take notes on the main character's feelings.

OK.

Can you **help** me, / **explain** that, / **say that** | **in German,** / **again,** / **repeat that,** / **spell** that word, / **write** this **on the board,** / **give an example,** **please?**	helfen / erklären / auf Deutsch sagen / noch einmal / wiederholen / buchstabieren / an die Tafel schreiben / Beispiel nennen
Can **I** **ask a question,** / **open a window,** / **switch on the light,** / **go to the toilet,** **please?**	Frage stellen / Fenster öffnen / Licht einschalten / zur Toilette gehen
Can we **do** **one more** / **another** **exercise**, please?	eine weitere Übung machen
What **'s the time.** / **'s that in German,** / does that **mean,** / **do we have to do** now, / **page are we on,** **please?**	Wie spät …? / Was bedeutet das auf Deutsch? / bedeuten / Was sollen wir nun machen? / Auf welcher Seite …?
Sorry, I **'m late.** / **haven't** **got** | **my homework.** / **that exercise.** / **my workbook** with me. / **finished yet.** / **'m not sure, if that is** | **correct.** / **right.**	zu spät kommen / Hausaufgabe / Übung / Arbeitsbuch / (noch nicht) fertig sein / nicht sicher sein, ob etwas richtig ist
I **feel ill.** / **have a** | **headache.** / **stomach ache.** / **don't feel well.**	sich krank fühlen / Kopfschmerzen / Bauchschmerzen / sich nicht wohl fühlen
Can **I** **work with** you, Dennis? / **borrow** / **have** **your** **ruler,** / **pen,** / **biro,** / **felt tip,** **please?** / you **pass** me the **ink eraser,**	zusammenarbeiten / ausleihen | Lineal / Füller / Kugelschreiber / Filzstift / Tintenkiller geben
Take out / **Close** your books, please!	herausnehmen / schließen
Please **open** your books **at** (BE) / **to** (AE) page 24. / **We're on** / **Turn to**	auf einer Seite öffnen / sich auf einer Seite befinden / Seite … aufschlagen

Who would like to	come to the board?			zur Tafel kommen
	write on the transparency?			auf die Folie schreiben
	take part in a role play?			an einem Rollenspiel teilnehmen
	play the part of the shop assistant?			eine Rolle übernehmen

Look at the picture and describe	what's happening	there.	was gerade geschieht
	who's doing what		wer was macht

Say it
Put it | in your own words, please! — mit eigenen Worten sagen

Give information about the	colours.	Farben
	time of day.	Tageszeit
	time of year.	Jahreszeit

Sum up the text, — zusammenfassen

Skim | the text for | general ideas, | please! — flüchtig lesen, überfliegen
Scan | | specific information, | — absuchen

Let's	sing along with the chorus!	den Refrain mitsingen
	play a game!	Spiel spielen
	make four teams!	vier Mannschaften bilden
	perform the dialogue.	einen Dialog spielen
	act out the scene!	eine Szene nachstellen

Speak	up,	Sprich bitte (ein wenig) lauter!
	a bit louder,	
	more clearly,	Sprich bitte deutlicher!
Be quiet,		please! — Ruhe bitte!
No prompting,		Bitte nicht vorsagen!
Don't interrupt,		unterbrechen
Could you stop chatting to your neighbour and listen,		aufhören sich mit dem Nachbarn zu unterhalten

It's your turn, Simon!		Du bist dran!
Find	a partner!	einen Partner finden,
Choose		auswählen
Work in	pairs!	Partnerarbeit
	groups!	Gruppenarbeit
Make groups of five!		Gruppen bilden
Form a	circle!	Kreis
	semi-circle!	Halbkreis
Take your chair	with you!	mitnehmen
	back!	zurückbringen

Make appointments with	ein Gespräch vereinbaren
Talk to	different partners in your group! — mit Gruppenmitgliedern sprechen
Have a discussion about school sponsoring!	diskutieren
Take turns!	sich abwechseln

Take notes!		schriftlich festhalten
Check		überprüfen
Compare │ **with** │ another team!		vergleichen
Swap cards │ │ your partner!		Karten austauschen
Hold up your cards!		Karten hochhalten

Throw the dice!		würfeln
Circle │		einkreisen
Underline │ the irregular verbs!		unterstreichen
Fill in the gaps!		Lücken füllen

Colour │ the pictures!		ausmalen
Match │ the pictures **with** the new words from the text!		zuordnen

Hang │ │ **in the classroom!**		im Klassenraum aufhängen
Put │ the poster │ **up** │ **on the wall!**		an der Wand aufhängen

Let's **take a short break** and continue in five minutes!   eine kurze Pause machen

Well done, Caroline!   Gut gemacht!

That's │ **very good!**   Sehr gut!
        │ **excellent!**   Ausgezeichnet!

You can do better, try again!   Das kannst du besser, versuche
                      es noch einmal!

For further phrases see also Chapter 10 *Giving feedback*.

v5yg3g

Hello, Lotus Restaurant, how can I help you?

Hello, good afternoon, I'd like to reserve a table for this coming Saturday.

Fine, I'd be happy to help you with that. How many guests will be in your party?

There'll be five of us.

What time would you like the reservation for?

Seven o'clock.

OK, that's a table for five on Saturday the 12th at seven o'clock. May I have your name, please?

...

This chapter will focus on the differences between private calls and business calls. Some expressions can be used in both situations, but most of them are used either in a private or in a business context.

3.1 Private calls – Privatgespräche

Taking a call – Einen Anruf entgegennehmen:

Hello.   Hallo!

Making contact/introducing yourself – Vorstellung:

Hi, **is that** Fiona?	
Hello. **Is that** Sheffield 57876?	ist dort
Hi, John, **this is** Peter Quinn.	hier spricht
This is Peter Quinn speaking.	
Is Neil there **by any chance?**	zufällig
Could I speak to Neil, please?	Könnte ich mit … sprechen?
I'd like to speak to Neil.	Ich möchte mit … sprechen.

Asking for information – Um Information bitten:

Who's calling, please?	Wer ist dran?
Who's speaking, please?	wer spricht
Is that Tony speaking?	Spricht dort Tony?

Asking the caller to wait – Bitten zu warten:

Just a moment, please.	
OK, **just a minute**, please.	einen Moment
Hold on, please.	bleib dran
Hang on for a sec. *(inf)*	bleib kurz dran

Problems – Probleme:

I'm afraid **you've got the wrong number.**	die falsche Nummer gewählt haben
Are you sure you have the right name?	Bist du dir sicher, dass das der richtige Name ist?
The **line is very bad.**	Die Verbindung ist sehr schlecht.
The **line is breaking up.**	Die Verbindung bricht ab.
We were cut off.	Wir wurden unterbrochen.
I can't speak right now. Could you **call back** later?	zurückrufen
I'm talking on the other line. I'll **ring you back** in a minute.	dich zurückrufen
Could you **speak up**, please?	lauter sprechen
Could you **repeat that**, please?	wiederholen

Taking a message – Eine Nachricht entgegennehmen:

Can I **take a message**?	eine Nachricht entgegennehmen
Would you like to **leave a message**?	eine Nachricht hinterlassen
No, thank you. I'll **call again later**.	später noch einmal anrufen

Leaving a message – Eine Nachricht hinterlassen:

Could you **give Mary a message**?	etwas ausrichten
Could you **ask Tim to call me back**?	bitten, mich zurückzurufen
Could you **tell her that I called**?	sagen, dass ich angerufen habe

---

Especially in spoken American English, conditional sentences are often shortened and tense usage is simplified. Example: "You come, we'll talk about it" for "If you come / came, we'll / we'd talk about it."

3.2 Business calls – Geschäftliche Telefonate

Taking a call – Einen Anruf entgegennehmen:

Good afternoon. Gearbox Solutions. **How can I help you?**	Wie kann ich Ihnen behilflich sein?

Making contact / introducing yourself – Vorstellung:

Hello. Is that Oxford 98432?	Hallo. Ist dort …?
Good afternoon. This is Mrs Jones. Could I **speak to** Mr Morgan, please?	sprechen
Could you put me through to Customer Service, please?	Können Sie mich durchstellen
This is Tracy from the NHS. I'm **returning your call** from this morning.	zurückrufen

Asking for information – Um Information bitten:

Can I ask who's calling?	Darf ich fragen, wer am Apparat ist?
What are you calling about?	Weshalb rufen Sie an? / Worum geht es?
What is your **reason for calling** us today?	Anlass für Anruf

Asking the caller to wait – Bitten zu warten:

Please **hold the line**.	dran bleiben
Hold on, please.	warten Sie
Just a moment, please.	einen Augenblick
I'm trying **to connect** you.	verbinden
One moment please, I'll **put you through**.	durchstellen

Problems – Probleme:

I'm afraid you've got **the wrong number**.	die falsche Nummer
Sorry, I think you've **dialled the wrong number**.	verwählt
Are you sure you have the right name?	Sind Sie sich sicher
I'm afraid Mr Smith no longer works here. I'll put you through to his **replacement**, Ms Jones.	Nachfolger

I'm afraid the line's **engaged**.	besetzt
I'm afraid Mr Morgan is in a **meeting** at the moment.	Besprechung
The **line** is very bad.	Verbindung
Could you **repeat** that, please?	wiederholen
Could he **call** you **back later**?	später zurückrufen

Taking a message – Eine Nachricht entgegennehmen:

Can I take a message?	Kann ich etwas ausrichten?
Would you like to leave a message?	Möchten Sie eine Nachricht hinterlassen?

Buying time – Sich Zeit verschaffen:

I'm afraid the line is very bad. Could you **try again** in five minutes?	nochmal versuchen
I'm sorry, but I have to rush off to a meeting. **Could I call you back** in an hour or so?	Kann ich Sie zurückrufen?
I'm afraid **now is not a very good time**. Could you call back in an hour, please?	gerade passt es nicht so gut

Leaving a message – Eine Nachricht hinterlassen:

Could you **give** him / her **a message?**	etwas ausrichten
Could you ask him / her **to call** me **back?**	zurückrufen
Could you **tell him / her that I called?**	jmd. ausrichten, dass ich angerufen habe
No, thank you. **I'll call again later.**	Ich rufe später noch einmal an.

tq72s8

Good morning, I'm Philippa Owen. We spoke on the phone.

Good morning, my name is Matt Lucas. Pleased to meet you, Mrs Owen.

Do take a seat please, Mr Lucas. Did you find us easily?

No problem at all. The directions your secretary gave me were really helpful.

Glad to hear that. Well, let's get down to business then. Why do you want to work for our company?

Well, I researched into your company before sending my application and I was very impressed by what I read. It would be a great privilege for me to work for you.

...

You can find other useful phrases for job interviews in chapter 9 Oral exams.

4.1 Starting a job interview – Ein Bewerbungsgespräch beginnen

Interviewer

Good morning,		
Good afternoon,	I'm Phil Owen. We spoke on the phone.	Guten Morgen
How do you do?		Guten Tag

Applicant

Good morning,		
Good afternoon,	I'm Matthias Kempen. Pleased to meet you,	Guten Morgen
How do you do?	Mr Owen.	Guten Tag

Interviewer

Take a seat, please, Mr Kempen.   Nehmen Sie bitte Platz.

Applicant

| **Thank you for inviting me,** | | |
| **Thanks for the invitation,** | Mr Owen. | Danke für die Einladung. |

Interviewer

Did you	have a good **journey** here?	Anfahrt
	find us **easily**?	gut/leicht finden
How was your **journey** here today?		Anfahrt

Applicant

The journey was	**smooth,**	thank you.	reibungslos, ohne Probleme
	fine,		
The **directions** your secretary gave me were really helpful.			Anfahrtsbeschreibung

Interviewer

			(Bemerkung zum guten Wetter)
Quite a	**warm**	day, isn't it?	warm
	sunny		sonnig

Applicant

Yes, we're really **lucky with** the weather, aren't we?	Glück haben mit
Yes, the weather's **lovely**.	gut
Yes, it's a **lovely day**.	schöner Tag

Interviewer

			(Bemerkung zum schlechten Wetter)
	cold		kalt
Quite a	**rainy**	day, isn't it?	regnerisch
	foggy		neblig

Applicant

Well, I've read it's **worse** in the south.	schlimmer
They're even expecting **floods**.	Überschwemmung
Never mind – it's good for my vegetables.	egal, macht nichts
At least it's not too windy.	wenigstens, zumindest
I hear it'll **clear up** later.	aufklaren

> In formal situations, such as a job interview, avoid reduced forms such as *gonna*, *gotta*, *wanna*, and, especially, *innit* for *isn't it*.

4.2 Talking about reasons for a job application – Über Bewerbungsgründe sprechen

Interviewer

Why do you want to work for this **company?**	Unternehmen
our **organization?**	Organisation
Why did you **apply for** this job?	bewerben auf

Applicant

I **researched** your company before	recherchieren
submitting my application.	einreichen
I was very **impressed** by what I read about the company.	beeindruckt
Your company's Facebook page is really **impressive**.	eindrucksvoll
My **dream** is to work in a company ...	Traum
It would be a great **privilege**	Privileg
... where I can **improve** my **skills**.	Fähigkeiten verbessern
... that is one of the best **employers** in the UK.	Arbeitgeber
This seems like a **fantastic** place to work.	fantastisch

Interviewer

Why are you **applying for** this particular **job?**	sich bewerben um
	Arbeitsstelle, Job
position?	Stellung, Posten
Why are you leaving your **current** job?	jetzig, gegenwärtig
Why do you want to **move on?**	sich beruflich verändern

Applicant

I see this job as a new **challenge.**	Herausforderung
opportunity.	Chance, Gelegenheit
This position offers an excellent **chance** to ...	Chance, Gelegenheit
I'm looking for a **change** that allows me to ...	Veränderung
... learn more about **retailing**.	Einzelhandel
... provide first-class **customer service**.	Kundendienst
... **broaden** my knowledge of business administration.	erweitern
I want to **explore** other opportunities.	erkunden
There wasn't **room for growth** with my previous firm.	Entwicklungspotenzial
I'm looking for a job with more **responsibility**.	Verantwortung

I was **laid off** because of a takeover.	gekündigt werden
I had to move back to this area due to personal **circumstances**.	Umstände
I've been working as a **temp** but I'm looking	Aushilfskraft, Zeitarbeiter
for a **permanent job** now.	Festanstellung

4.3 Talking about education and job experience – Über Ausbildung und Berufserfahrung sprechen

Interviewer

What	are / were	your **favourite subjects** at school?	Lieblingsfächer

Applicant

I suppose my favourite subject	is / was	**history** / **science** / **Latin**	because	Geschichte / Naturwissenschaften / Latein
		... I'm interested in our local **heritage**.		Erbe, Tradition
		... I enjoy understanding **natural phenomena**.		Naturphänomene
		... it's the **basis** for many other languages.		Grundlage

Interviewer

Tell me about your **qualifications**.	Qualifikationen
Why do you believe you are **qualified** for this job?	geeignet, qualifiziert

Applicant

I **took** my **Abitur** last year.	Abitur machen
I've got a **bachelor's degree** in business studies.	Bachelor-Abschluss
I did my **apprenticeship** at Debenhams.	Berufsausbildung

Interviewer

What relevant **work experience** do you have?	Berufserfahrung

	grammar school?	Gymnasium
	comprehensive school?	Gesamtschule
What have you done since leaving	**vocational school?**	Berufsschule
	university?	Universität
	your **previous** job?	vorherig

Applicant

After my **gap year** in Australia ...	Jahr zwischen Schule und Universität
After **graduating** from university ...	absolvieren
Before my **employment gap** ...	Zeitraum ohne Beschäftigung
... I spent three months on a **work placement** in Spain.	Praktikum
... I took a **course** in webdesign.	Kurs
... I worked in **Purchasing** at Burberry's for two years.	Einkauf(sabteilung)

4.4 Talking about personal background – Über Persönliches / Privates sprechen

Interviewer

How would you **describe**	yourself?	beschreiben
	your **personality**?	Persönlichkeit

Tell me a bit **about** yourself.   erzählen … von
How would your friends and **colleagues** describe you?   Kollegen

Applicant

I'd **describe** myself	as a person who is …	beschreiben
I guess they'd **characterise** me		charakterisieren

… **easy to get along** with.   umgänglich, unkompliziert
… **down-to-earth.**   bodenständig, realistisch
… an **efficient** team-player.   tüchtig, leistungsfähig
… **flexible** and **adaptive.**   flexibel … anpassungsfähig
… **self-motivated.**   eigenmotiviert
… **self-confident.**   selbstbewusst
… **focused.**   fokussiert
… **diplomatic.**   diplomatisch
… used to working under **pressure.**   Druck

Interviewer

It says here on your	**CV** *(BE)*	that you like martial arts.	Lebenslauf
	résumé *(AE)*		

Are you involved in any **extra-curricular** activities?   außerschulisch

	hobbies?	Hobbies
What are your	**interests?**	Interessensgebiete
	leisure activities?	Freizeitaktivitäten

What do you do in your **spare time?**   Freizeit

Applicant

When I have some **spare time** …
In my free time …   In meiner Freizeit
When I'm not working, …

	exercise.	Sport treiben
… I like to	**do karate.**	Karate machen
	spend time with my family.	Zeit mit der Familie verbringen
	go trainspotting.	Züge beobachten

	a **keen**	begeistert
I'm	a **dedicated**	photographer.	passioniert
	an **amateur**	Amateur-

4.5 Dealing with tough questions – Mit schwierigen Fragen umgehen

Interviewer

	strength?	Stärke
What is your greatest	**weakness?**	Schwäche
	achievement?	Leistung

Applicant

Actually, I can't **think of** a real weakness.   einfallen

Okay, I might sometimes be a bit | **impatient.**   ungeduldig
| **bossy.**   rechthaberisch
| **perfectionist.**   perfektionistisch

To be honest, I used to
struggle with   sich mit etw. schwer tun

speaking in public, …   in der Öffentlichkeit reden
meeting deadlines, …   Termine einhalten
working on several **projects** at the same   Projekt
time, …

… but my | **communication skills** have | Kommunikationsfähigkeit
| **organizational skills** have | greatly improved …   Organisationsfähigkeit
| **time management** has | Zeitplanung
… after my employer provided **in-service training**.   innerbetriebliche Fortbildung

I guess my greatest strength is my ability to …

… work with people **from different backgrounds**.   unterschiedlicher Herkunft
… focus on **the job at hand**.   die aktuelle Aufgabe
… complete a project **ahead of schedule**.   schneller als geplant
… to listen to my clients' **concerns**.   Sorgen, Belange

Interviewer

Why should we **employ** you?   einstellen
Why do you believe you are **qualified** for this job?   geeignet, qualifiziert
Do you think you could **fit into** a company like ours?   zu etw. passen

Applicant

I feel | I possess | all the **requirements** | for the position.   Voraussetzung, Anforderung
| I have | the drive **required** | nötig, erforderlich
This job **seems like** an ideal **match** for my skills and experience.   scheint zu passen zu
I'm used to working with foreign **clients**.   Kunden
I believe I have the right **attitude** and skills for the role.   (mentale) Einstellung, Haltung
I have all the skills you're **looking for**.   suchen

Interviewer

Where do you see yourself five years from now?   Wo sehen Sie sich in fünf
Jahren?

Applicant

Within five years, I would like to …

… have developed my **leadership skills**.   Führungskompetenzen
… have more **responsibility**.   Verantwortung
… lead a team of two or three **buyers**.   Einkäufer
I see myself **progressing** in my field.   weiterkommen
In five years I hope to be working as a **team leader**.   Gruppenleiter
My **long-term** goals involve gaining more experience.   langfristig
I can see many challenges **lying ahead of me**.   vor jmd. liegen

4.6 Providing information for the job applicant – Dem Bewerber Informationen geben

We're a	**leading**		führend
	medium-sized		mittelständisch
	large		groß
	family-owned		in Familienbesitz
		manufacturer of textiles.	Hersteller
		supplier of IT products.	Lieferant
		export company.	Exporteur
		import company.	Importeur
		retailer.	Einzelhändler
		wholesaler.	Großhändler
		chain store.	Ladenkette
		hotel chain.	Hotelkette

Our	**factory**		Fabrik, Fertigungsstätte
	plant		Werk, Betrieb
	headquarters	is located in York.	Zentrale, Hauptstandort
	department		Abteilung
	subsidiary		Filiale, Zweigstelle
	charity		Wohltätigkeitsorganisation

Our business was	**founded**	in 2012.	gründen
	established		gründen, aufbauen
	set up		eröffnen

We	**specialize in**		sich spezialisieren auf
	mainly **deal with**		es zu tun haben mit
	focus on		sich konzentrieren auf
	concentrate on		sich konzentrieren auf
		car **manufacturing.**	Herstellung
		the **distribution of goods.**	Warenverteilung
		providing **customer service.**	Kundendienst

Our	**company philosophy** is	based on three principles.	Unternehmensphilosophie
	mission statement is		Unternehmensleitbild
	corporate values are		Unternehmenswerte
We're **committed** to			verpflichtet sein
	our **founder**'s vision.		(Firmen-) Gründer
We're really proud of our	social	**commitment.**	Engagement, Verpflichtung
	environmental		

4.7 Questions to ask the interviewer – Fragen an den Interviewer stellen

Interviewer

Do you have any questions **Is there anything you would like**	**to ask us?**	Haben Sie noch Fragen?

Applicant

Where would I be located? — Wo würde ich arbeiten?
Who would I be reporting to? — Wer wäre mein Vorgesetzter?
What **staff training** would be available? — Mitarbeiterschulung
When can I **expect** to hear from you? — erwarten
What kind of **salary** could I expect in this position? — Gehalt

I'm going to need more information about …

… my **initial pay**.	Einstiegsgehalt
… my **starting salary**.	Einstiegsgehalt
… my **working hours**.	Arbeitszeiten
… the **fringe benefits** │ your company provides.	freiwillige Sozialleistungen
… the **perks**	zusätzliche Leistungen
… your company **policy** on smoking.	Regeln

Would it be possible for me to work …

… **part time**?	in Teilzeit
… **full time**?	in Vollzeit
… **flexitime**?	in Gleitzeit
… **shifts**?	im Schichtdienst

Would I	be expected to **travel**?	reisen
	get **travelling expenses**?	Reisekosten
	get a **holiday allowance**?	Urlaubsgeld

4.8 Closing the job interview – Das Vorstellungsgespräch abschließen

Interviewer

Is there anything you would like to **add**? — hinzufügen

Thank you for	**coming in today.**	Danke für Besuch
	your interest in our company.	Danke für Interesse

When could you start to work for us? — Wann könnten Sie bei uns
When would you be available? — anfangen?
You will hear from us **shortly**. — bald

Applicant

Thank you so much for giving me this **opportunity**. — Chance
What will the next steps in the **hiring process** be? — Einstellungsverfahren

I could start work	**immediately**.	sofort
	at one month's **notice**.	mit einer Frist von

So, today I told you a bit about homelessness in, erm, Britain. Are there any questions?

Yes. Here. You mentioned that there are programmes to help people find jobs or earn some money. What are they?

Ah yes, of course. One of the best examples is probably 'The Big Issue', a magazine sold on the street by homeless people. Any other questions?

You mentioned homeless children. Are there any exact numbers?

Well, there's obviously a large grey area, but the charity 'Shelter' reckons that around 90,000 children are going to be homeless this Christmas. This includes children in temporary accommodation.

...

During a presentation, you should structure your information as clearly as possible in order to keep your audience with you. Let them know when you are moving on to a new point or section. And, especially, point out to your audience in advance when they can ask questions.

5.1 Stating the topic – Angabe des Themas

The **topic** of this presentation is	the role of women in India.	Thema
My presentation **deals with**		behandelt

5.2 Giving an overview at the beginning – Themenüberblick

I've **structured** my presentation as follows:		gliedern
My presentation **is divided** into	four main parts.	unterteilt
My presentation **is in**		besteht aus

First, a general overview of the situation of women in India.	erstens
Second, the historical background.	zweitens
Third, three recent cases of violence against women.	drittens
Finally, the activities of human rights groups.	schließlich

5.3 Signposting – Markierung der verschiedenen Aspekte

	give you a **concrete** example.	konkret
Let me	**quote** an Indian politician here.	zitieren
	remind you of what I said before.	erinnern

This **leads** me to		bringen
	turn to	zuwenden
I'd like to	**move to**	my next point.	weitermachen mit
Now to		nun zu

5.4 Using visuals – Verwendung visueller Mittel

For further phrases see also chapter 9.2.3 Visual material: graphs and diagrams.

	graph		Graph, Kurve
This	**chart**	shows reported cases of violence against women.	Tabelle
	map		Landkarte

As you can **conclude**,				schlussfolgern
It becomes	**obvious**			offensichtlich
	evident	that	the number has sharply risen.	klar
You can **clearly see**				klar sehen, erkennen
These statistics **reveal**				offenbaren

5.5 Referring to a previous point – Rückverweise

You may **recall** that I mentioned the rise in reported cases.			sich ins Gedächtnis rufen
As I mentioned	**earlier on,**	many cases remain unreported.	zuvor
	at the outset,		eingangs

5.6 Dealing with problems related to technology or time – Mit Problemen (Technik oder Zeit) umgehen

Can you all hear me? I'll try to **speak loudly.**		laut sprechen
I'm afraid we have a problem	with the **microphone.**	Mikrofon
	because the **projector** isn't working.	Beamer
Please **refer to**	your handouts.	benutzen
	pages 5 and 6.	

We're running out of time, so I'll just	**skip to** the end.	übergehen zu
	finish here.	beenden, Schluss machen

5.7 Answering questions – Entgegennahme von Fragen

	pleased			gerne bereit
I'd be	**glad**	to answer your questions	now.	froh
			as I go along.	während des Vortrages
Please	**hold** questions **back** until the end of my presentation.			zurückhalten
	feel free to ask at any time.			fragen Sie ruhig

5.8 Giving a summary – Zusammenfassung

Well, **that**	**'s** about **it** for today.		das war's
	was the last **section** of my presentation.		Abschnitt
To	**sum up,**	I've talked about four main points.	zusammenfassend gesagt
	summarize,		

5.9 Thanking the audience – Dank an die Zuhörer

Thank you very much for your **attention**.	Aufmerksamkeit
It's been a **pleasure** talking to you.	Vergnügen
answering your questions.	

a5iq3b

In my opinion, cannabis should be legalized.

Why do you think so?

Well, first of all it's used for medical purposes and surely, if it was legal, the crime that's associated with it right now would be reduced a lot.

I'm afraid I don't agree at all. If you legalize cannabis, then the first thing that'll happen is that people will be screaming for other drugs to be legalized too, such as ecstasy…

That's not necessarily true. Cannabis and ecstasy are two completely different types of drug.

…

6.1 Expressing and defending your opinion – Die eigene Meinung vertreten

In my opinion,		meiner Meinung nach
In my view,		meiner Ansicht nach
To my mind,	cannabis should be legalized.	meiner Meinung nach
The way I see it,		so wie ich das sehe
I don't think		ich denke nicht, dass

First of all,		zunächst einmal
To begin with,	taxes are too high.	erstens
Next, I'd like to **point out** that		darauf hinweisen

What's more,	the oil price is falling again.	außerdem
Moreover,		außerdem

The same	**holds true for**	personal property taxes.	trifft zu auf
	is relevant for		ist von Belang

To sum up,		zusammenfassend gesagt
In brief,	I reject this plan.	kurz gesagt
In sum,		mit einem Wort
To put it briefly,		um es kurz zu sagen

6.2 Expressing agreement and disagreement – Zustimmung und Ablehnung ausdrücken

OK, you may	**be right**	there.	Recht haben
	have a point		etwas könnte dran sein
There may be	**some truth in**	what she said.	etwas Wahres daran

	certainly **thought-provoking.**	ein Denkanstoß
What John said is	**broadly** correct.	weitgehend
	true **as far as it goes.**	zunächst einmal, so weit

	true **up to** a certain	point.	bis zu
		degree.	Grad
		extent.	Maß
That's		**level.**	Ebene
	wrong in	some **respects.**	Hinsicht
		many **ways.**	
	irrelevant **as far as** the US **is concerned.**		was …. betrifft

---

Contractions:
In spoken English it is common to use short forms. For example:
    he is → he's
    you are → you're
    he does not → he doesn't

Somehow you haven't managed to	**get** your point **across.** **convince** me.	klar machen überzeugen

What you say	**isn't** | **necessarily** so. **isn't** | **invariably** the case. **stretches things a little bit.** is only **partly** true. is **slightly exaggerated.** isn't **one hundred percent** accurate. **sounds** | **convincing.** **sounds** | **self-evident.** **sounds** | **perfectly clear.**	notwendigerweise ausnahmslos (leicht) übertreiben teilweise leicht übertrieben hundertprozentig klingt einleuchtend selbstverständlich sonnenklar

Yes, **that's true** I do see your point,	**but** | let's avoid generalisation. **but** | there's more to it.	zwar wahr, aber das ist nicht alles

OK, but	that certainly **doesn't** | **mean** | that this has always that certainly **imply** | been so. **on the other hand** many Americans profit from it. I'm **not quite so sure.**	heißt nicht bedeutet nicht andererseits nicht so sicher

I would I'd	**question** **challenge** your second argument. **object to**	in Frage stellen anfechten ablehnen, widersprechen

That's true / right.	Das stimmt.
Exactly.	
Precisely.	Genau!
You | 're right.	hast Recht
You | 've hit the nail on the head. *(coll)*	den Nagel auf den Kopf getroffen

I | agree completely with you.	übereinstimmen
I | couldn't agree more that wind energy doesn't solve any problems.	unbedingt zustimmen
I | don't think so either.	auch … nicht

Not at all.	
No way. *(coll)*	keineswegs

I | disagree.	nicht zustimmen
I | beg to differ.	anders denken
I | wouldn't say so.	nicht so denken
I | can't make head nor tail of what you say. *(coll)*	nicht schlau werden

Oh, come on, that's	a	gross exaggeration.		krass
		completely different topic.		Thema
	beyond	the point.		am Thema vorbei
	not			gehört nicht zur Sache
Sorry, but in my book, what you say is		unconvincing.		meiner Ansicht nach
				nicht überzeugend
		inappropriate.		unangebracht
		polemical.		unsachlich

These arguments	do not	work.		zutreffen
		hold	water. (coll)	stichhaltig sein
			up.	
	are flawed.			fehlerhaft

You	've been	playing down the cost of these reforms.	herunterspielen
		twisting my words.	verdrehen
		presenting a distorted picture of the situation.	verzerrt
	underestimate the side effects of this new pill.		unterschätzen

6.3 Explaining and emphasizing your ideas – Die eigenen Gedanken erklären und ihnen Nachdruck verleihen

To put it	simply,	I do not share this view at all.	kurz gesagt
	boldly,		unverblümt
	bluntly,		offen gesagt

Let me	give you an example.	Beispiel
	make this clear. I do not support this plan.	klarstellen

What	's most important	is that this war should stop.	am wichtigsten
	really matters		zählt

In my view, what is most	disturbing	is the increase in taxes.	beunruhigend
	telling		aufschlussreich

I think	we're	really	in need of a complete change of policy.	benötigen
		quite definitely		ganz bestimmt
	that's exactly what we need.			genau

6.4 Solving problems of communication – Missverständnisse beseitigen

Excuse me(,)	I didn't	catch that.	mitbekommen
		quite understand that.	verstehen
	could you speak up a bit?		lauter sprechen
	for interrupting you.		unterbrechen

What exactly do you **mean by**		verstehen unter
Could you **define**		definieren
Would you mind explaining the meaning of	"distorted"?	könntest du bitte
Is **that what** you mean by		ist es das, was

If I understand you **correctly**, you're against this plan. richtig
Would you mind **elaborating on** that? näher erläutern

	saying	that there should be higher taxes on books?	behaupten
	implying		nahelegen
Are you	**suggesting**		
	proposing		vorschlagen

Oh, I see. Ach so.
Now I **see.** verstehen
 agree. zustimmen

6.5 Changing the topic – Das Thema wechseln

In this **context,**			Zusammenhang
By the way, *(inf)*	it's necessary	to talk about the costs.	übrigens
For that matter,			übrigens auch
	we **mustn't** forget		dürfen nicht

Perhaps we could	**return to**	that later.	wieder aufgreifen
	get back to		zurückkommen auf

	take into consideration.	berücksichtigen
There is something else that we should	not **overlook.**	übersehen
	deal with.	behandeln

If we could, I'd like to **move on to** the topic of immigration. weitermachen mit

Today we're here to discuss whether mobiles should be banned in schools. If you could please outline your arguments for a ban, Peter? Then after that we can hear the arguments against such a ban.

OK. Well first of all, the use of mobiles in schools is going to cause a lot of disruptions to lessons.

And what is your view on the ban, Jen?

Well, I don't think mobiles should be banned. They should be turned off during lessons, but not banned altogether. For parents, being able to know where their child is, is a good thing. Also, the children can let their parents know if they're going to be late or if there's an emergency.

Peter, would you want to respond to this?

...

Chairing a discussion is a demanding task since it means keeping the discussion going by encouraging everyone to participate and, at the same time, ensuring that none of the participants dominates the discussion. Of course, time management is of crucial importance.

7.1 Getting the discussion started – Die Diskussion eröffnen

OK, shall we	**open** **start**	the discussion?			eröffnen

So, today we're	**looking**	at into	the issue of child labour.	beschäftigen uns mit untersuchen
	considering			betrachten

The issue we're looking at is	highly very	**complex.** **controversial.** **contentious.**	vielschichtig kontrovers
		disputed.	umstritten
		sensitive.	heikel
		international **in scope.**	im Ausmaß
		an **unresolved** matter.	ungeklärt

The situation The issue at hand	has	become the **focus** of media attention. **led to heated debate.**	Blickpunkt hitzige Diskussionen auslösen

The	**initial question** **central issue**	is whether mobiles should be banned in school.	Ausgangsfrage Hauptthema

We should	**be clear** about **agree** on explain **precisely**	what we mean by child labour.	im Klaren sein uns einigen genau

7.2 Keeping the discussion going – Die Diskussion am Laufen halten

Any	**alternatives?**		Alternativen
	conclusions?		Schlussfolgerungen
	corrections?		Richtigstellungen
	diverging opinions?		abweichende
	further		weitere
		comments?	Kommentare
		evidence?	Beweismaterial
	other	**implications?**	Auswirkungen
		measures?	Maßnahmen
	objections?		Einwände
	solutions?		Lösungen
	suggestions?		Vorschläge

| Peter, do you want to | comment on
expand
respond to
add a little more to
come in here?
pick up on this point? | that view? | kommentieren
ausführen
reagieren auf
hinzufügen
hierzu etwas sagen
aufgreifen |

| Can we move on to | talk about
sharing information? | a related issue
a different approach
the economic dimension | now? | damit zusammenhängend
Ansatz
Dimension
austauschen |

| So we can draw | a parallel
an analogy | to the situation in China. | Parallele
Vergleich |

| Thanks, Peter. Does everyone | follow that?
share Peter's view?
think this is a balanced view? | nachvollziehen
teilen
ausgewogen |

Can I just quickly **recap** your point? — kurz zusammenfassen

| Let me | go back to
rephrase
put it differently. | the question. | zurückkommen auf
umformulieren
anders ausdrücken |

7.3 Encouraging everyone to participate – Jeden zur Teilnahme ermuntern

| Janet, you've made quite a few interesting points so far, but could I just ask if anyone else wants to | come in here?
contribute something?
speak their mind? | Ideen beisteuern
sich einschalten, hierzu etwas sagen
beitragen
Meinung sagen |

| Would anyone like to | come up with a different suggestion? (inf)
disagree?
question this view? | beisteuern, vorschlagen
widersprechen
in Frage stellen |

Is there anyone who has**n't** spoken **yet**? — noch … nicht

7.4 Avoiding getting sidetracked – Verhindern, dass man vom Thema abkommt

| I'm sorry but that's | not the issue.
beyond the point. | Thema
gehört nicht zur Sache |

We should	avoid	getting sidetracked.	vom Thema abkommen
		getting stuck on this point.	steckenbleiben
		losing the thread.	den Faden verlieren
		losing ourselves in details.	Einzelheiten
	try to keep to the point.		bei der Sache bleiben

7.5 Keeping the discussion fair – Dafür sorgen, dass die Diskussion fair bleibt

Let's try to	avoid	generalisations.	Verallgemeinerungen
		unnecessary repetitions.	unnötige Wiederholungen
		stereotypes.	Klischees
		stereotyping.	den Gebrauch von Klischees
	not	mince words.	Klartext reden
		dramatise things.	dramatisieren
	stick to the facts.		sachlich bleiben

7.6 Managing the time and summing up – Die Zeit richtig einteilen und die Diskussion zusammenfassen

Sorry, but I think	we're running out of time.		uns geht … aus
	we need to	round off	abschließen
		finish	beenden
		this discussion soon.	
	that's about as far as we can take this discussion.		führen

| Would anyone like to make any final points? | abschließende Bemerkungen |

| OK, it looks like we've covered quite a | lot of ground. | weiter Bereich |
| | range of views on this topic. | Bandbreite |

| Can we | leave it at that? | darauf beruhen lassen |
| | agree to differ? | akzeptieren, dass es unterschiedliche Standpunkte gibt |

| So, are we all | agreed on | this solution? | einverstanden mit |
| | happy with | this outcome? | zufrieden mit |

| So most of us | believe | that cell phones should be banned in school. | verbieten |
| | hold | | sind der Überzeugung |

Is that	an adequate		angemessen
	a comprehensive	summary?	umfassend
	an unbiased		unvoreingenommen

| Obviously, various questions have remained | unanswered. | unbeantwortet |
| | elusive. | schwer in den Griff zu bekommen |

rg2m9c

Excuse me, could you do me a favour, please? I don't quite understand what the writing on this traffic sign means.

Sounds like you could do with some help. If you like, I can translate for you.

Oh, yeah, that would be nice of you.

Now, let me see: it says: overtaking of tractors and slow-moving vehicles is allowed.

Sorry, I didn't quite understand what you said. Could you repeat that, please?

Of course. Let me put it this way: no overtaking except when there is a tractor or a slow-moving vehicle. Got it?

Oh yes, now I know what you mean. Thank you for helping me.

8.1 Asking for help with language problems – Um Hilfe bitten bei Sprachproblemen

Could you **do** me a **favour**? — Gefallen tun

| I don't quite understand | **what this sign says.** | was auf diesem Schild steht |
| | **what this sign means.** | was dieses Schild bedeutet |

You **don't happen to speak German, do you?** — Sprechen Sie zufällig deutsch?

| **Do you think you could** | help me with this ticket machine? | Könnten Sie mir wohl …? |
| **Would you be so kind as to** | | Wären Sie so freundlich …? |

How do you say 'Praktikum' in English? — Wie sagt man …?
What do you call a 'Schnitzel' in English? — Wie nennt man …?
What's the word for 'Riesenrad' in English? — Wie heißt das Wort für …?
I'm not familiar with the meaning of 'Ey up me duck'. — … ist mir nicht geläufig
What does the 'V sign' **stand for**? — bedeuten, stehen für

8.2 Offering help with language problems – Hilfe anbieten bei Sprachproblemen

Can I be of any assistance? — Kann ich irgendwie helfen?
If you need help with the manual, **just let me know.** — sagen Sie einfach Bescheid
Sounds like you could **do with** some **help**. — Hilfe brauchen

I hope I can be of help to you. *(fml)* — Hoffentlich kann ich Ihnen behilflich sein.

I'm a **native speaker** of English. — Muttersprachler
English is my **native language** — Muttersprache
If you like, I can **translate** for you. — übersetzen
I guess I might be able to help you with the paperwork. — Ich schätze, ich könnte Ihnen helfen

8.3 Checking for understanding – Das Verständnis überprüfen

Could you	**repeat** that, please?	wiederholen
	say that **again**, please?	noch einmal sagen
	explain what you mean by that?	erklären

I didn't quite catch what you said. — Ich habe Sie akustisch nicht verstanden.

Sorry, I've never heard that **expression** before. — Ausdruck

What do you mean by that? — Was meinen Sie damit?
I can't quite follow. — Ich kann nicht ganz folgen.
I'm not familiar with the meaning of …. — … ist mir nicht geläufig
What I want to say is … — Was ich sagen will, ist:
Let me put it this way … — Lassen Sie es mich mal so sagen:

| Do you know | **what I mean?** | was ich meine |
| | **what I'm saying?** | was ich sagen will |

(Have you) got it? *(inf)* — Hast du es (verstanden)?

8.4 Reporting what people say – Berichten, was Leute sagen

> Mediating spoken language does not mean you give a word-for-word translation of what someone says, but rather try to convey the gist of the message. For this purpose, the use of so-called reporting verbs can be helpful:
>
> **Example:**
>
> Text in direct speech:
> ***I'm really sorry*** *I couldn't make it in time for the meeting. It won't happen again!*
>
> Mediated text:
> *He **apologized** for being late.*

He **assumes** you're the only one who can help him.	annehmen, vermuten
She is **wondering** how she can get back to England without her passport.	sich fragen, sich Gedanken machen
She **suspects** she lost it on the train.	vermuten, einen Verdacht hegen
He doesn't **approve of** the way he's been treated.	billigen, akzeptieren
It's hard for him to **admit** he's too old for the job.	zugeben, eingestehen
He seems to **agree with** your idea.	zustimmen
She **welcomes** your plan in general, but **refuses** to get personally involved.	begrüßen … ablehnen
They **deny** all charges made against them.	leugnen

	declines	ablehnen
As far as I can tell, he	**rejects** your offer.	ablehnen
	accepts	akzeptieren, annehmen

She wants to **complain about** a member of your staff.	sich beklagen, sich beschweren
He is **complaining about** how he was treated at the check-in.	sich beschweren über
He would like to **apologize for** the trouble he caused.	sich entschuldigen
She **advises** you to save your money.	raten, den Rat geben
They want to **invite** you to their wedding next month.	einladen
He's **offering** to help you with the suitcases.	anbieten
She has **decided** to book a return flight.	sich entscheiden, beschließen
He **insists on** paying the bill for you.	bestehen auf
What she **recommends** is that you keep silent about this.	empfehlen, vorschlagen
He can **suggest** a good restaurant in the neighbourhood.	empfehlen
He wants to **congratulate** you on your exam results.	gratulieren
They **claim** to have seen you in the shopping centre.	behaupten
She **refuses** to believe her flight is cancelled.	sich weigern
He **doubts** they will ever come back here again.	zweifeln
He's trying to **warn** us about the thunderstorm.	warnen

Reported Speech:

Mediating in spoken scenarios is often similar to **reported speech**. If the reporting verb (e.g. *say, ask, want to know* etc.) is in the past tense, the tenses of the *that-clause* are backshifted, i.e. present tense in direct speech is turned into past tense in reported speech, present perfect in direct speech is turned into past perfect in reported speech, etc. Please note that adverbials of time and place (e.g. *here, now, today*) are not changed because speaking and mediating take place in the same communicative situation.

8.5 Paraphrasing and summarizing – Umschreiben und Zusammenfassen

In plain English, **In other words**	this means you're fired.	im Klartext mit anderen Worten
That means **That is to say**	he won't give us any support.	das bedeutet, das heißt
A better way of putting it is he's my favourite singer.		um es besser auszudrücken
There are two problems, **namely** money and time.		nämlich, und zwar
Basically, **Essentially,**	his parents are broke.	im Grunde
In short, **In brief,**	he's an absolute beginner.	kurz gesagt kurz gesagt
In a nutshell, **To sum it up,** **To cut a long story short,**	he's got some trouble with his parents.	kurz gesagt, zusammengefasst
So, what you're saying is you can't help us? **What I want to say is …** **Let me put it this way …** **Let me put it like this …**		Sie wollen also sagen … Was ich sagen will, ist: Lassen Sie es mich mal so sagen:
All in all, he seems to miss his family. **On the whole,** I'd say he regrets his decision.		alles in allem insgesamt, im Großen und Ganzen
By and large, **The bottom line is**	he doesn't care about his image.	im Großen und Ganzen im Endeffekt
In any case, **Anyway,**	there's nothing we can do about that now.	jedenfalls, auf alle Fälle

af3kw2

Hello, can I sit here?

Yes, sure. Please, sit down! You're the guy from Germany who's taking part in our exchange program, aren't you? We're on the same course in Math. I'm Cathy.

Pleased to meet you, Cathy. I'm Tom from Hamburg in Germany. I've only been here for two weeks now. I'm still having a few problems finding my way round the school building.

Yeah, it's quite a big school, isn't it? There are about 1200 students on the campus. So it must be very confusing for you at the beginning.

Well, the most confusing thing is getting to the classrooms on time. I didn't know that all the teachers have got their own room. It seems I always have to hurry along the corridors.

...

You can find other useful phrases in chapter 4 Job interviews.

9.1 Warming up – Aufwärmphase

Good	morning, afternoon,	Lisa, Ben,	**sit down,** **take a seat,**	please!

Nimm bitte Platz!

How are you? — Wie geht es dir?
Are you feeling ok?
This is my **colleague**, Britta Weiß. Have you met before? — Kollegin

| Can you please **introduce yourself** | **briefly**? | kurz vorstellen |
| | **in a few words**? | mit einigen Worten |

First we'd like **to get to know sth about** you. — erfahren, besser kennenlernen
Where do you **live**? — wohnen, leben
What are your **favourite subjects**? — Lieblingsfächer
How long have you been **learning English**? — Englischunterricht haben
Have you ever been to **countries where English is spoken**? — im englischsprachigen Ausland
What do you **plan to do** after your *Abitur*? — planen, vorhaben

Good morning, Mr/ Mrs Schwarz, **I'm fine**, thank you. — Mir geht es gut.
My name is Julia Schneider. — Ich heiße
I **was born** in Munich. — geboren sein

I've been living here since 2002. — wohnen, leben

		15 years old.		Ich bin 15
		pupil	Lessing School.	Schüler, Student
I'm	a		at	**student**	Max-Weber-Berufskolleg.	Schüler an weiterführenden Schulen
		in **year** 10.		Klasse, Jahrgangsstufe

I've been learning English for five years now. — seit … Englischunterricht haben

| Before we start, | do you **have any questions?** | Fragen haben |
| | is there **anything you're not sure about?** | sich nicht sicher sein |

Sorry, I'm not quite sure if I **understood you correctly**. — richtig verstehen
Excuse me, I didn't **catch** the last part of the question. — verstehen, erfassen

Could you	**rephrase** that,	please?	anders / neu formulieren
	repeat that,		wiederholen
	say that again,		
	speak more slowly,		langsamer sprechen
	explain what you mean by the word …,		erklären

| Who | would like to **begin?** | |
| | wants to **get the ball rolling?** *(inf)* | anfangen |

Let's start with you, Sam!

Now	**let's hear** what Sarah has to say about her topic!		hören
	it's your turn, Mike!		Du bist an der Reihe!
Right, over to you now, Laura!			Nun zu dir …

You've been	**looking at**	a photo of ….	anschauen
	preparing	sth on the topic of school uniforms.	vorbereiten
I assume you've had **sufficient time** for the assignment.			ausreichend Zeit
You're asked to	**describe**	a cartoon, aren't you?	beschreiben
	analyse		analysieren
	point out		herausstellen
	focus on		konzentrieren auf
Please,	**compare**	the two major arguments!	vergleichen
	contrast		gegenüber stellen
	discuss		diskutieren, erörtern
	comment on		Stellung nehmen zu
Make use of your **notes**!			Stichwörter, Notizen
Look at the **keywords** you've underlined!			Schlüsselbegriffe

Please, take one of the **role cards**!		Rollenkarten
Imagine you are the person described on your card!		sich vorstellen
Adopt	**his / her point of view!**	seine / ihre Perspektive annehmen
Argue from		argumentieren

I've been given a short quote by Aldous Huxley.		mir wurde vorgelegt
Let me start by saying a few words about the author.		
I'm going to start by telling you what the text is about.		beginnen
I'd like to	**begin** with the eye-catching photo.	
	give you a short overview of the main points.	einen kurzen Überblick geben
The **subject of my talk** is racism in football.		Thema des Vortrags
There are four **points I'd like to make.**		Punkte herausstellen
First I'd like to say sth about the lack of security.		zunächst
After that I'll explain the message of the photo.		anschließend
Then I'll deal with the diagram.		dann
Finally, I'll comment on the most recent developments.		schließlich

9.2 Dealing with different sources – Unterschiedliches Quellenmaterial bearbeiten

9.2.1 Presenting a text – Einen Text präsentieren

When you present a text as part of an oral exam, make sure that you differentiate between the answers. Keep them separate and present each of them in a clearly structured way.
In summaries, line references or quotations are not usually given. In the other answers it is necessary to do so.
As far as summaries of fictional texts are concerned, the present tense group is used. Sometimes students make the mistake of using the past tense group looking back at a story or novel that was read in class.

The text I've been given	**is** **was written**	**by** John Miller.	stammt von wurde verfasst
The article at hand	**was published** **came out**	in April 2014.	wurde veröffentlicht

The text is	**taken** **an excerpt** **an extract** **a passage**	**from** scene 6 of *The Glass Menagerie* by Tennessee Williams.	wurde entnommen Auszug Abschnitt

It	**deals with** **'s about** **discusses** **questions**	the planned cuts in the education budget.	behandeln handeln von diskutieren, erörtern in Frage stellen
The **topic** is			Thema
The	**purpose** **aim**	of the article is to alert the readers.	Absicht Ziel

The article	**can be divided into** **consists of**	four paragraphs.	aufteilen in bestehen aus
	is structured as follows.		folgendermaßen strukturiert
	is a **typical example of** a human interest story.		typisches Beispiel

I'm going to start by **giving a short summary**. — kurze Zusammenfassung geben

My first task is to **summarize** the text. — zusammenfassen
I'm also supposed to analyse the language used by the author. — Außerdem soll ich …

I'd like to	**move on to** **get on with** *(inf)*	the next question.	fortfahren, weitermachen
Let's continue with			
Now to			nun zu

My last task is to **comment on** the author's view. — Stellung nehmen zu

Last but not least, I'd like to present my own view. — zu guter Letzt, schließlich

The author **starts by stating** that internet crime is a very serious problem. — beginnt mit der Aussage
At the beginning of the article we learn sth about crimes committed via social-networking sites. — am Anfang
Next, we're given the latest statistic figures. — anschließend
Then the author **goes on to** give several examples. — fortfahren
In the last part of the article he comes to a conclusion. — im letzten Teil

The article	**ends** **finishes** **concludes**	**with** a look into the future.	abschließen mit

The author	**quotes** various sources.		zitieren
	includes quotes from several experts.		Zitate einbeziehen

The quotations are given in	**direct**	**speech.**	direkte Rede
	indirect		indirekte Rede

	backs up		bestätigen
The following quote	**supports**	the author's theory.	unterstützen
	corroborates		erhärten

We can see this		Dies ist zu erkennen …
This can be seen	in line 14.	
An example of this is		Ein Beispiel hierfür ist …

The author **underlines** his point with several arguments.   unterstreichen

In the second	**refers to**		sich beziehen auf
paragraph she	**alludes to**	the Prime Minister's speech.	anspielen auf
Then she	**brings up**		zur Sprache bringen
	broaches	the topic of global warming	
	mentions		erwähnen
He then	**raises the question of**	what to do now.	Frage aufwerfen
	talks about		sprechen über

	formal		formell
The text is written in	**informal**	English.	informell
	everyday		Alltags-(Englisch)
	colloquial		umgangssprachlich

	serious.	ernst
	matter-of-fact.	sachlich
The tone of the article is	**humorous.**	humorvoll
	ironic.	ironisch
	critical.	kritisch
	conciliatory.	versöhnlich

	mostly uses	**simple**	sentences.	einfach
		complex		komplex
The author	employs many **rhetorical devices.**		Stilmittel
	also includes	**slang expressions.**	Slangausdrücke
		vulgar terms.	vulgäre Ausdrücke
		jargon.	Fachsprache

Both in spoken and written English, it is perfectly correct to use the pronouns *they / their / them* instead of the clumsy *he* or *she / him* or *her / his* or *her(s)*.
Examples: "Has anybody lost **their** car key?" – "Someone might wonder where **their** car key is." – "It's an excerpt from a parent's letter to **their** child."

9.2.2 Presenting visual material: pictures and film – Bildmaterial präsentieren: Bilder und Film

What we've got here is This is	a colour photo.	Farbfoto
	a black-and-white drawing.	Schwarzweißzeichnung
	a cartoon.	Karikatur, Cartoon
	a still.	Standbild
	an oil painting by Picasso.	Ölgemälde
	a portrait of Charles Dickens.	Portrait
	an advert for a fitness drink.	Anzeige
	the cover of a novel by Nick Hornby.	Buchumschlag, Titelbild

In the	picture photo	you can see Manhattan.	auf dem Bild Foto
The picture	shows of is	the Eiffel Tower. full of detail.	zeigen detailliert

It's a **colour** picture. — vollfarbig

The colours are	bright. dark.	hell dunkel

The cartoon was **drawn** by Pat Oliphant.	zeichnen
	machen
This photo was · probably **taken** · in Miami.	auf, bei
· obviously **staged**. · at a party.	gestellt

The cartoon was **drawn** by Pat Oliphant. — zeichnen

This photo was	probably **taken** obviously **staged**.	in Miami. at a party.

zeichnen
machen
auf, bei
gestellt

The picture has definitely been	touched up. photoshopped.	retuschiert mit Photoshop nachbearbeitet

There's	a child sitting an old man standing a group of young people	in the	foreground. background. centre. middle.	Vordergrund Hintergrund Mitte
		on the	left. right.	links rechts

At the	top bottom	of the picture there's a horse.	oben unten
In the	top bottom	right-hand left-hand	corner, we can see a tree.	oben rechts unten links
Next to			neben
To the	left right	of	the stage there's a camera operator.	links neben rechts neben

The	top half upper bottom lower	third part	of the picture is blue.	obere Hälfte oberes Drittel unteres Drittel unterer Teil

The focus is on the girl with the skateboard. — Augenmerk, Blickpunkt

Westminster Bridge is	seen **from**		below.	unten
			above.	oben
The Houses of Parliament are		**the**	front.	vorne
			back.	hinten

There's a sharp **contrast between** light and dark. Kontrast zwischen

If we take a closer look	we find a deeper message.	bei eingehender Betrachtung
At second glance		auf den zweiten Blick

There are many details that **contribute to** the message of the photo. beitragen zu

I was **deeply moved** when I saw the photo. tief bewegt, ergriffen
My first thought was that we must react right away. mein erster Gedanke
My second thought is that we have to consider the circumstances mein zweiter Gedanke ist
  under which the photo was taken.

	picture	**reminds me**	**of** my last trip to Scotland.	erinnern an
		makes me think		denken lassen an
The	poster	**makes you think of** a perfect beach holiday.		Eindruck vermitteln
	atmosphere	created	by the picture is	**sombre.**	düstere Atmosphäre
	mood	evoked		**mysterious.**	geheimnisvolle Stimmung

The advert		cleverly made.	geschickt, klug gemacht
		amazing.	erstaunlich
		thought-provoking.	zum Nachdenken anregend
	is	very impressive.	sehr eindrucksvoll
The photo		disgusting.	abstoßend
		shocking.	schockierend
		hilarious.	urkomisch
The cartoon		highly controversial.	äußerst kontrovers

	combines a drawing with a text.	verbinden
		speech bubbles.	Sprechblasen
The cartoon	has	a very provocative **caption.**	Bildunterschrift
	picks on a current news event.	(aus kritischer Sicht) ein
		aktuelles Ereignis aufgreifen

		exaggeration.	Übertreibung
	makes use of	irony.	Ironie
		a pun.	Wortspiel
The cartoonist	employs **humorous elements.**	humorvolle Elemente
	is aiming at **a younger target group.**	jüngere Zielgruppe
	is very **sarcastic.**	sarkastisch
	criticises the new Education Bill.	kritisieren

The **scene** I've just seen is from

an	**action film**. *(BE)*	Actionfilm
	horror movie. *(AE)*	Horrorfilm
a	**comedy**.	Komödie
	commercial.	Werbespot
	YouTube video.	Videoclip von YouTube

This is an **episode from a TV series**. — Folge einer Fernsehserie

Szene

This **still** is taken from — Standbild

the beginning		(Film-)anfang
middle	of the film.	(Film-)mitte
end		(Film-)ende

The scene has an **important function within the plot**. — wichtige Funktion innerhalb der Handlung

	follows a short dance sequence.	… folgt im Anschluss an …
is	**followed** by a terrible accident.	Im Anschluss folgt …
a	**flashback**.	Rückblende
	flashforward.	Vorausblende

The camera takes a

long		Totalaufnahme
medium		halbnah
high-angle	shot.	Vogelperspektive
low-angle		Froschperspektive
eye-level		Normalansicht

The director uses **reverse-angle** shots. — über die Schulter
The scene starts with a **close-up** of the hero. — Nahaufnahme

The camera

zooms	**in on** the Indian woman's face.	heranfahren, heranzoomen
	out after the car has moved out of view.	herauszoomen
tilts	**down** to the foot of the hill.	nach unten schwenken
	up to the roof.	nach oben schwenken
pans	**in on** a boy playing in a sandpit.	horizontal schwenken
	from left to right.	von links nach rechts

The shots **follow each other** very quickly. — aufeinander folgen

This scene is shown in

slow	motion.	Zeitlupe
fast		Zeitraffer

There are only few **cuts**. — Schnitt

The **soundtrack** is made up of the — Soundtrack

dialogues,	Dialog
voice-over,	Erzählerstimme
music and	Musik
sound effects.	Geräuscheffekte

9.2.3 Presenting visual material: diagrams and graphs – Bildmaterial präsentieren: Schaubilder und Tabellen

This **diagram**	appeared		Diagramm, Schaubild
This **table**	was published	in The Economist of 7 May.	Tabelle
This **statistic**			Statistik
This **survey**			Übersicht
	is	**up-to-date.**	aktuell
		outdated.	veraltet
		reliable.	glaubwürdig, zuverlässig
		trustworthy.	vertrauenswürdig

This **line graph**	illustrates a common trend.	Linien-, Kurvendiagramm
This **vertical bar chart**	shows the figures for Wales.	Säulendiagramm
This **horizontal bar chart**	deals with EU petrol prices.	Balkendiagramm
This **pie chart**	describes a process.	Kreis-, Tortendiagramm
This **flow chart**	visualizes the structure of a sentence.	Flussdiagramm
This **tree diagram**		Baumdiagramm
This table consists of	five **columns.**	Spalten
	ten **rows.**	Zeilen, Reihen

	a **title,**	Titel
	a horizontal **time scale,**	Zeitskala
This diagram is made up of	a vertical **axis,**	Achse
	a **key,**	Legende
	a **grid,** and	Gitternetz, Raster
	coordinates.	Koordinaten
This pie chart is divided into	various **segments.**	Segmente, Abschnitte
	three **slices.**	Stücke, Anteile

The **shading**		Schattierung, Schraffierung
The **colour**	of the bars helps you to understand the chart.	Farbe
The **labelling**		Beschriftung
The **figures**		Zahlen, Zahlenangaben
The **numbers**	underline this development.	Zahlen
The **percentages**		Prozentsätze

	steady		stetig
	gradual		allmählich, schrittweise
	slow		langsam
	slight		geringfügig, leicht
This diagram shows a	**sharp**	increase in productivity.	scharf, stark
	significant		bedeutend, erheblich
	dramatic		dramatisch, drastisch
	considerable		beträchtlich
	massive		gewaltig

The line graph **suggests**			deutet auf …hin
	a sharp **rise** in	car prices.	Anstieg
	a slow **increase of**		Anstieg
	a strong **growth rate**.		Wachstumsrate
	an **upward** trend.		aufsteigend

	has **gone up**.	ansteigen
	has **risen**.	ansteigen, zunehmen
According to the table, CO2 output	has **increased**.	ansteigen, zunehmen
	has **grown**.	wachsen, steigen
	has **reached its peak**.	den höchsten Stand erreichen

	drop		
	decrease		
The statistic shows a	**decline**	in the number of car thefts.	Rückgang, Abnahme, Sinken
	reduction		

The dollar has hit an	**all-time low** against the euro.	tiefster Stand aller Zeiten

	went down as expected.	
Last year, profits	**fell** dramatically.	sinken, fallen, abnehmen
	dropped considerably.	
	decreased sharply.	

9.3 Role play – Rollenspiele

9.3.1 General strategies – Grundlegende Vorgehensweise

- Take a close **look at the information given** on your role card.
- If possible **take a few notes**. Consider all the relevant aspects: Where? When? Why? For what purpose?
- Your examiner will inform you about the situation you are to deal with. **If you have any questions, feel free to ask.**
- Look at your partners. **Smile, be friendly** and **polite** and **keep eye contact**.
- **Try to appear self-confident** and **use the right body language**. Sit upright in a relaxed manner and lean forward slightly.
- **Speak clearly** and **not too fast.**
- Make sure your voice doesn't become monotonous. **Stress keywords** and **pause at the end of important statements.**
- **Use words and expressions that you feel comfortable with.** Avoid particularly complex sentences and words whose meaning or pronunciation is not quite clear to you.

In Britain, most people tend to avoid gesticulation in polite conversation or in formal situations.

9.3.2 Situations and tasks – Situationen und Aufgaben

Applying for a holiday job – Sich um einen Ferienjob bewerben

> You're a German student applying for a summer job in a London hotel to gain some work experience. The applicant who gets the job will be expected to work in different areas of the hotel service. Use the QR-Code on page 54 to listen to a sample dialogue.

Useful vocabulary – Hilfreiches Vokabular

Thank you very much for	**inviting** me / **the invitation**	to this interview.	einladen / Einladung

This job offer	has **attracted my attention** because…		Aufmerksamkeit wecken
	really **appeals to** me.		ansprechen, reizen
	sounds	**very interesting.**	sehr interessant
		exciting.	aufregend
	is really **challenging.**		herausfordend

I've got	some **work experience** as a receptionist.		Berufserfahrung (auch in Form eines Praktikums)
	good	**teamworking** skills.	Teamfähigkeit
		communication	Kommunikationsfähigkeit
		language	Fremdsprachenkenntnisse
		computer	Computerkenntnisse
		people	gut mit Menschen umgehen können

I'm	**well-suited** for this job.	gut geeignet
	motivated and **keen to learn.**	motiviert; lernbereit
	a **team player.**	teamfähig
	a **reliable** person.	verlässlich
	responsible.	verantwortungsbewusst
	open-minded.	weltoffen, vorurteilsfrei
	cooperative.	kooperativ, hilfsbereit
	well-organized.	gut organisiert
	thorough and hard-working.	gründlich

You've probably read this in my	**CV.**	Lebenslauf
	letter of application.	Bewerbungsschreiben

I've added a **letter of recommendation.**	Empfehlungsschreiben

Dealing with everyday problems at an American high school – Mit alltäglichen Problemen an einer amerikanischen High School umgehen

> You're a German exchange student spending six months at South Oldham High School in Kentucky, USA. You're staying with an American host family. During the first weeks you get into a conversation in the lunch break with one of the regular South Oldham students who can help you with some of the problems you have.

Keith	**goes to** / **attends** / is a **student** at	Albany High School.	zur Schule gehen / eine Schule besuchen / Schüler

Most students come on the **school bus**. — Schulbus
Many 16-year-olds can already **drive to school by car**. — mit dem (eigenen) Auto fahren

The students have individual **schedules**. — Stundenplan
The first **period** starts at 8.15. — Unterrichtsstunde
Morning **recess** is at 10.00. — Pause
There's a **lunch break** between 11.55 and 1.15. — Mittagspause
Classes finish at 3.00. — Unterricht

There is a wide range of **subjects** / **courses** you can take. — Fach / Kurs
Some of them are **compulsory**. / **optional**. — verpflichtend / freiwillig

This semester I've chosen **Math**, (AE) / **Chemistry**, / **Social Studies**, / **Computer Science**. — Mathematik / Chemie / Gesellschaftswissenschaft / Informatik
A **career adviser** helps you organise your schedule. — Beratungslehrer/in

In the afternoon there are lots of **extra-curricular** activities. — außerunterrichtlich
Every high school offers a lot of **clubs**. / large **sports program** (AE). — Arbeitsgemeinschaften / Sportangebot
Many girls want to **join the cheerleaders**. — bei den Cheerleadern mitmachen
The **Student Council** is of major importance, too. — Schülervertretung
organises **charity events**. / the **Homecoming Dance**. — Wohltätigkeitsveranstaltung / großer Schulball mit Ehemaligen

Students	regularly meet	in the	lunch hall. / assembly hall.	Speisesaal, Mensa / Aula
	can work quietly		study.	Selbstlernzentrum; auch: Selbstbeschäftugung
	do a lot of sport		gym.	Sporthalle

Many American high schools have strict **rules**. / a **dress code**. — Regeln, Hausordnung / Kleiderordnung
At some schools students have to wear a **school uniform**. — Schuluniform

Students are always expected **to be**	**on time.**	pünktlich sein
	prepared.	vorbereitet
They aren't allowed to	**skip lessons.**	Unterricht schwänzen
	cheat in a test.	täuschen, schummeln

Bullying is strictly forbidden.   Mobbing
In some cases students even get **detention**.   Nachsitzen
Dave was very lucky to **pass the exam**.   Prüfung bestehen
Peggy was unhappy because she **failed**.   nicht bestehen, durchfallen
Not everybody got a good **grade** in the end.   Note

74q3dp

Wow! You did a great job! Your performance was very natural and authentic.

Thank you. It's good to hear that.

What I liked about your role-play in particular was your flexibility and the effort you put into your script. That was really impressive!

Yes, I also thought that worked well.

10.1 Giving positive feedback – Positives Feedback geben

Wow!	Toll!
Bravo!	Bravo!
Very good!	Sehr gut!
Well done!	Gut gemacht!
(You did a) Great job!	Toll gemacht!
Great stuff!	Tolles Zeug!
Awesome! *(AE)*	Toll! Fantastisch!
I like that.	So was mag ich.
Right!	Stimmt!
Quite right!	Stimmt genau!
Correct!	Richtig! Korrekt!
That's it!	Das ist es!
Perfect!	Ausgezeichnet! Einwandfrei!
Magnificent!	Großartig! Hervorragend!
Excellent!	Herausragend! Exzellent!
Fantastic!	Fantastisch!
Fabulous!	Großartig! Fabelhaft!
Exactly!	Genau!
Congratulations!	Glückwunsch
Congratulations on your presentation!	Glückwunsch zu …
That was a **clever** answer.	clever, schlau

	impressive.	eindrucksvoll
	outstanding.	hervorragend
	brilliant.	ausgezeichnet, glänzend
Your performance was	above average.	überdurchschnittlich
	very natural.	sehr natürlich
	authentic.	glaubwürdig
	faultless.	makellos, fehlerfrei,
	flawless.	einwandfrei

That was	straightforward.	schnörkellos
	very **comprehensive**.	umfassend, umfangreich

I'm	impressed!	beeindruckt
	amazed!	erstaunt

What I really liked about your role play was your creativity. — was mir wirklich gefallen hat an

That's just what I was looking for. — Genau das habe ich erwartet.

You put a lot of effort into your speech. — viel Mühe in etw. stecken
What strikes me is your flexibility. — was mir auffällt, ist …

There's nothing wrong with your answer. — es gibt nichts auszusetzen
an …

Not bad!	Nicht schlecht!
You're halfway there.	Du hast die Hälfte geschafft.
You've almost got it.	Du hast es fast geschafft.
You were almost right.	Es stimmte beinahe.
You're on the right track.	auf dem richtigen Weg
You've got the idea.	Du hast es verstanden.
You've got the message.	Du hast es verstanden.

10.2 Giving negative feedback – Negatives Feedback geben

> When you are giving negative feedback, it may sometimes be necessary to be direct and straight-forward (see the expressions that follow this box).
> Here are two strategies to express criticism in a milder, more polite way:
> 1. The negative tone of a statement may be softened by using expressions like *a little, a bit, a little bit, slightly, rather, somewhat.*
>
> **For example:**
>   *The diagrams in your presentation are a little confusing.*
>   This sounds much more diplomatic and polite than:
>   *The diagrams in your presentation are confusing.*
> 2. A similar softening effect can be achieved by including expressions like *I'm afraid, so sorry, to be honest, unfortunately,* which help to convey the speaker's empathy with the person that is being criticised.
>
> **For example:**
>   *I'm afraid the examples you gave were not convincing.*
>   This sounds much more diplomatic and polite than:
>   *The examples you gave were not convincing.*

Terrible!	Schrecklich! Furchtbar!
Awful!	Grässlich!
Hopeless!	Hoffnungslos! Aussichtslos!
Lousy!	Lausig!
Miserable!	Erbärmlich! Kläglich!
What a nuisance!	
How annoying!	Wie ärgerlich!
That was a **feeble** joke.	schwach
Your speech was **lacking in ideas.**	ideenarm
Your argumentation was **extremely poor.**	äußerst schwach, äußerst dürftig
Expectations were high, but delivery was **mediocre.**	mittelmäßig, durchwachsen
The illustrations you chose were **unsuitable.**	ungeeignet
The applicant seemed rather **incompetent.**	inkompetent
Your behaviour was **completely unacceptable.**	völlig inakzeptabel
The answer you gave me was **inadequate.**	unzulänglich, mangelhaft
The use of tenses in your essay was **incorrect in parts.**	teilweise falsch

That was not what I expected.			Es war nicht das, was ich erwartet hatte.
That was really **disappointing**.			enttäuschend
You should have told me sooner.			Das hätten Sie mir früher sagen sollen.

I	noticed observed	that the diagrams were	**missing** references. **confusing**. **inappropriate**.

Mir ist aufgefallen, …
Ich habe beobachtet, …
es fehlte an …
verwirrend
unangemessen

10.3 Suggesting improvements – Verbesserungsvorschläge machen

The presentation could have been	**more interactive.** **more detailed.**	interaktiver ausführlicher

Don't worry about your		Machen Sie sich keine Sorgen um
	accent.	Akzent
	pronunciation.	Aussprache
	punctuation.	Zeichensetzung

I suggest that you leave out slides 4 and 7.	Lassen Sie besser … aus
What I would suggest is you doublecheck your notes.	Ich würde vorschlagen
Perhaps there could have been fewer colloquial expressions.	Vielleicht hätte es weniger … geben sollen
Why not try something new **next time?**	Warum versuchen Sie beim nächsten Mal nicht …?
What about interviewing your classmates?	Wie wäre es, wenn …?
Have you considered using a microphone?	Haben Sie mal darüber nachgedacht …
Why don't you look it up in your dictionary?	Warum … nicht?
In the future you might take some notes.	In Zukunft könnten Sie
Let's turn this **negative** experience into something positive.	negativ

10.4 Receiving feedback – Feedback entgegennehmen

Thanks for the feedback you gave me. **Thank you for taking the time to give me feedback.**	für Feedback danken
It's good to hear that.	Es ist gut, das zu hören.
Thanks for reminding me.	Danke, dass Sie mich erinnert haben.
Yes, I also thought that worked well.	Ja, ich dachte auch, dass das gut geklappt hat.
That's a good idea, I hadn't thought of that.	Das ist eine gute Idee, daran hatte ich nicht gedacht.
Can you tell me what you think would work better?	Können Sie mir denn sagen, was besser funktionieren würde?
Do you have any **suggestions**?	Vorschläge, Anregungen
I'm not quite sure I understand what you're saying.	Ich weiß nicht so genau, ob ich verstehe, was Sie sagen wollen.
When you said my performance was inadequate, **what exactly did you mean?**	…, was genau meinten Sie damit?
Can you describe what makes me appear arrogant to you?	Können Sie beschreiben, was mich Ihrer Meinung nach arrogant wirken lässt?
So the main thing I should focus on is my body language?	Ich sollte mich also hauptsächlich auf … konzentrieren.

11 Index

11.1 English – Alphabetisches Verzeichnis der englischen Stichwörter

11.2 German – Alphabetisches Verzeichnis der deutschen Stichwörter